Lerner SPORTS

★★★★★
SUPER SPORTS
TEAMS

INSIDE THE LOS ANGELES RAMS

JOSH ANDERSON

Lerner Publications ◆ Minneapolis

SPORTS THRILLS *MEET* RESEARCH SKILLS

Lerner SPORTS

Free Database Trial: **lernersports.com**

Lerner Publications Company
An imprint of Lerner Publishing Group, Inc.
241 First Avenue North
Minneapolis, MN 55401 USA

For reading levels and more information, look up this title at www.lernerbooks.com.

Main body text set in Aptifer Slab LT Pro / Typeface provided by Linotype AG

Library of Congress Cataloging-in-Publication Data

Names: Anderson, Josh, author.
Title: Inside the Los Angeles Rams / Josh Anderson.
Description: Minneapolis, MN : Lerner Publications, [2024] | Series: Lerner sports. Super sports teams | Includes bibliographical references and index. | Audience: Ages 7–11 | Audience: Grades 4–6 | Summary: "When the Rams moved to Los Angeles, California, in 2016, they instantly became one of the most high-profile teams in the NFL. Learn about the history and future of the defending Super Bowl champions"— Provided by publisher.
Identifiers: LCCN 2022049765 (print) | LCCN 2022049766 (ebook) | ISBN 9781728491011 (library binding) | ISBN 9798765604045 (paperback) | ISBN 9798765601594 (ebook)
Subjects: LCSH: Los Angeles Rams (Football team : 2016–)
Classification: LCC GV956.L6 A64 2024 (print) | LCC GV956.L6 (ebook) | DDC 796.332/640977866—dc23/eng/20221024

LC record available at https://lccn.loc.gov/2022049765
LC ebook record available at https://lccn.loc.gov/2022049766

Manufactured in the United States of America
1 – CG – 7/15/23

TABLE OF CONTENTS

CHAMPIONS ONCE MORE 4

A TEAM ON THE MOVE 9

AMAZING MOMENTS. 15

RAMS SUPERSTARS 19

LET'S GO, RAMS!. 25

Rams Season Record Holders 28
Glossary. 30
Learn More 31
Index 32

Odell Beckham Jr. catches a touchdown pass in the 2022 Super Bowl.

CHAMPIONS ONCE MORE

FACTS AT A GLANCE

- The **RAMS** started in Cleveland, Ohio, in 1937.

- From 1999 to 2001, fans called the team's offense the **GREATEST SHOW ON TURF**.

- Wide receiver **COOPER KUPP** had 1,947 receiving yards in 2021. That's the second-most receiving yards ever gained in a single National Football League (NFL) season.

- The Rams won their second **SUPER BOWL** in 2022.

In 2022, the Los Angeles Rams became only the second team to compete in a Super Bowl played on its home field. After winning the National Football Conference (NFC) Championship Game, the team earned a spot in the 2022 Super Bowl against the Cincinnati Bengals. The game took place at SoFi Stadium near Los Angeles, California.

The Rams struck first when quarterback Matthew Stafford threw a 17-yard touchdown pass to wide receiver Odell Beckham Jr. Los Angeles had the lead at halftime. But the Bengals pulled ahead in the third quarter.

The Rams trailed 20–16 going into the closing moments of the game. They had the ball at their own 21-yard line with about six minutes left in the fourth quarter. In an amazing 15-play drive, the

Rams marched all the way down the field. With less than two minutes to go, they lined up for a play just outside the end zone.

Cooper Kupp, the best Rams wide receiver, stood across from a Bengals defender on the right side of the field. Stafford took the ball and turned in Kupp's direction. The quarterback tossed the ball while Kupp was still turned away from Stafford. Kupp looked back just in time. He spun around, leaped into the air, and cradled the ball against his chest. He fell to the ground in the end zone for a touchdown.

Cincinnati failed to score in the final seconds, and the Rams won 23–20. They became Super Bowl champions for the second time in team history. Kupp won the game's Most Valuable Player (MVP) award. He finished the Super Bowl with eight catches and two touchdowns.

Cooper Kupp (*right*) finished the 2022 Super Bowl with 92 receiving yards.

Kupp leaps into the air for the game-winning touchdown catch.

Quarterback Bob Waterfield led the Rams to the 1945 NFL Championship.

A TEAM ON THE MOVE

The Rams started in Cleveland, Ohio, in 1937. Team official Damon "Buzz" Wetzel was a fan of college football's Fordham University Rams. Wetzel suggested the name to Homer Marshman, the team's owner. Marshman liked the sound of the name and agreed.

Cleveland Stadium was the first home field for the Rams.

The Rams played their first eight NFL seasons in Cleveland. During that time, the team played in three different stadiums. Their only winning season in Cleveland was their last one. The Rams won the 1945 NFL Championship. In 1946, the team left Cleveland for Los Angeles. The Rams became the first major professional sports team in California.

Left to right: Corby Davis, Rudolph Mucha, Johnny Drake, and Parker Hall played for the Rams during the team's early years.

Left to right: Woody Strode, Jackie Robinson, and Kenny Washington in their college football uniforms

Racist policies by team owners kept Black players out of the NFL between 1927 and 1945. Before the team's first season in Los Angeles, the Rams added Black players Kenny Washington and Woody Strode. The Cleveland Browns signed two Black players that year as well. The four men played their first NFL season in 1946 and marked the end of the league's racist rules.

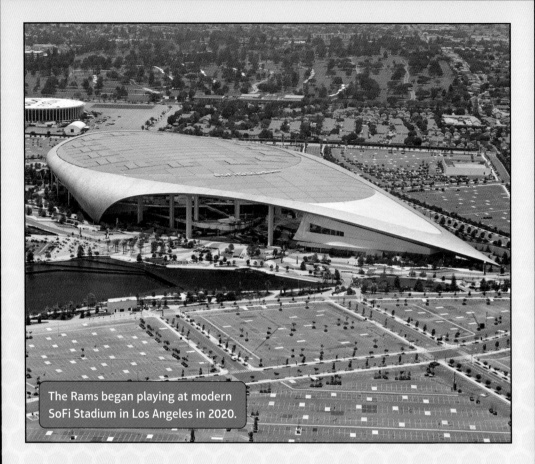

The Rams began playing at modern SoFi Stadium in Los Angeles in 2020.

The Rams failed to win an NFL Championship for many years, but they often made the playoffs. They were especially good in the 1970s and 1980s. In the 1990s, Georgia Frontiere, the team's owner, wanted to build a new stadium in southern California. When she couldn't get the support she needed, she moved the team to St. Louis, Missouri. The Rams played there for 21 seasons. In 2000, the team won its first Super Bowl.

The Rams moved back to Los Angeles in 2016. Since their return to the West Coast, the Rams have played in the Super Bowl twice. In 2020, the brand-new SoFi Stadium became their home. The Rams share SoFi with another NFL football team, the Los Angeles Chargers.

Marshall Faulk led the Rams in rushing six times when the team played in St. Louis.

Quarterback Kurt Warner tries to avoid Tennessee Titans defenders during the 2000 Super Bowl.

AMAZING MOMENTS

No matter where they've played, the Rams have had many amazing moments. After seven losing seasons, they defeated Washington 15–14 for their first NFL Championship in 1945. They won another in 1951.

The Rams of the late 1960s had one of the league's best defenses. The team's defensive line was called the Fearsome Foursome. The group helped the Rams win 10 or more games every year from 1967 to 1969. In 1973, the team hired coach Chuck Knox. During Knox's five years with the Rams, they won the NFC West every season.

The Rams made it to their first Super Bowl in 1980. But they lost to the Pittsburgh Steelers 31–19. It took the Rams 20 years to make it to the Super Bowl again.

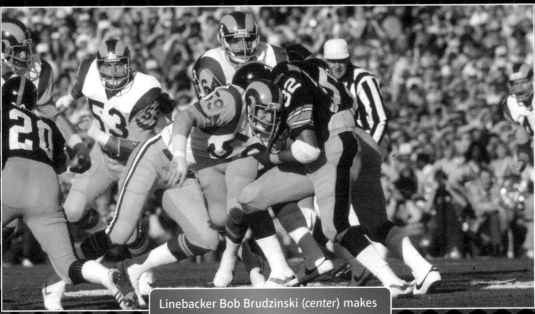

Linebacker Bob Brudzinski (*center*) makes a tackle during the 1980 Super Bowl.

From 1999 to 2001, the Rams scored the most points in the NFL. Fans called their high-powered offense the Greatest Show on Turf. The team's high-scoring style helped them reach the 2000 Super Bowl. Their opponent was the Tennessee Titans.

The 2000 Super Bowl is best remembered for the last play of the game. The Rams were ahead 23–16, but the Titans had a chance to score on the game's final play. From the 10-yard line, the Titans quarterback connected with wide receiver Kevin Dyson. Dyson caught the ball and ran toward the end zone. As he reached forward with the ball, Rams linebacker Mike Jones tackled him. Dyson was one yard short of the end zone. Time ran out, and the Rams finally had their first Super Bowl victory.

The Greatest Show on Turf made it back to the Super Bowl in 2002. But this time, the Rams lost to the New England Patriots 20–17.

Kevin Dyson reaches for the end zone during the last play of the 2000 Super Bowl.

The Rams hired Sean McVay as their head coach in 2017 after missing the playoffs for 12 straight seasons. McVay led the Rams back to the playoffs in his first year. The team returned to the Super Bowl in 2019. But they lost to the Patriots 13–3. Fans would have to wait until 2022 to see the Rams win their second Super Bowl.

RAMS FACT

The Rams got within one win of the Super Bowl three years in a row from 1974 to 1976. Each time, they lost in the NFC Championship Game.

Sean McVay has led the Rams to a winning record each season since joining the team in 2017.

Defensive end Deacon Jones (*right*) was a member of the NFL's 100th Anniversary All-Time Team.

RAMS SUPERSTARS

The Rams have had many superstar players and coaches in the team's long history. Quarterback Roman Gabriel played for the team in the 1960s and 1970s. He led the Rams to 74 wins in his 11 seasons. Gabriel led the NFL in touchdown passes in 1969. He won the NFL MVP award that year.

Quarterback Roman Gabriel led the Rams to the playoffs twice.

Merlin Olsen was a member of the Fearsome Foursome defensive line that led the Rams to several successful seasons in the late 1960s. He was a Pro Bowl player 14 times. Another member of the Fearsome Foursome was Deacon Jones. Sacks were not kept as an official statistic when he played. But Jones ranks third all-time on the NFL's unofficial list of sack leaders. Both Olsen and Jones were on the NFL's list of the 100 greatest players of all time.

Jack Youngblood played defensive end for the Rams in the 1970s and 1980s. He led the league in sacks twice. Youngblood played every game of the 1979 playoffs and the 1980 Super Bowl with a broken leg.

Merlin Olsen (*center left*) specialized in sacking quarterbacks in the 1960s and 1970s.

Eric Dickerson rushed for 56 touchdowns during his time with the Rams.

Several great running backs have played for the Rams. Eric Dickerson ran for 2,105 yards in 1984, setting an NFL single-season record. The Hall of Fame player led the NFL in rushing yards in three of his four full seasons with the Rams. From 2005 to 2012, running back Steven Jackson ran for more than 1,000 yards every season. Todd Gurley was another star running back for the Rams. Gurley led the league in rushing touchdowns in 2017 and 2018.

Wide receiver Isaac Bruce runs for a touchdown in a 2000 game against the Green Bay Packers.

Jackie Slater played 20 seasons on the offensive line for the Rams from 1976 to 1995. Not long after Slater retired, the Rams chose his replacement with the first overall pick in the NFL Draft. Orlando Pace played for the team from 1997 to 2008. Both players are now members of the Pro Football Hall of Fame.

Quarterback Kurt Warner was the engine behind the Greatest Show on Turf offense that helped the team reach two Super Bowls. He won the league's MVP award twice during his six seasons with the Rams. One of Warner's top targets was Isaac Bruce. The Hall of Fame wide receiver ranks fifth all-time with 15,208 receiving yards.

Sean McVay became the youngest head coach in NFL history when the Rams hired him in 2017. He was only 30 years old. McVay led the team to 55 regular season wins in his first five seasons in Los Angeles. The team made the playoffs in four of those years.

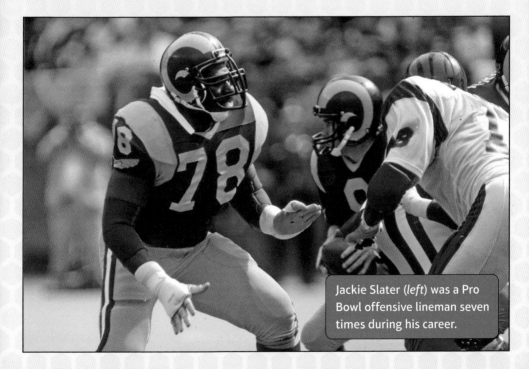

Jackie Slater (*left*) was a Pro Bowl offensive lineman seven times during his career.

Quarterback Matthew Stafford looks for an open receiver during the 2022 Super Bowl.

LET'S GO, RAMS!

The Rams traded for quarterback Matthew Stafford before the 2021 season. Head coach Sean McVay hoped his new passer would jumpstart the Rams offense. Stafford had played his first 12 seasons with the Detroit Lions. In his first year with the Rams, Stafford set team records with 4,886 passing yards and 404 completed passes.

Stafford is surrounded by talented teammates that include wide receiver Cooper Kupp. In 2021, Kupp led the NFL in both receiving yards and touchdown catches. His 1,947 yards were the second-most ever in a single NFL season.

Kupp catches a pass during a game against the Dallas Cowboys.

The Rams are equally strong on defense. Defensive lineman Aaron Donald has won the NFL's Defensive Player of the Year award three times. He is one of the best to ever play his position. Cornerback Jalen Ramsey is one of the toughest defenders in the league. He has been a Pro Bowl player in each of the last five seasons.

Before the 2022 season, the team signed future Hall of Fame linebacker Bobby Wagner. Wagner was a key part of the Seattle Seahawks defense that allowed the fewest points in the NFL every year from 2012 to 2015. The Rams also added wide receiver Allen Robinson. Robinson had never played with a quarterback as talented as Stafford before coming to Los Angeles. The moves should make an already strong team even better.

The Rams have all the pieces they need to compete for another NFL championship. After tasting victory in the 2022 Super Bowl, fans and players in Los Angeles are hungry for more.

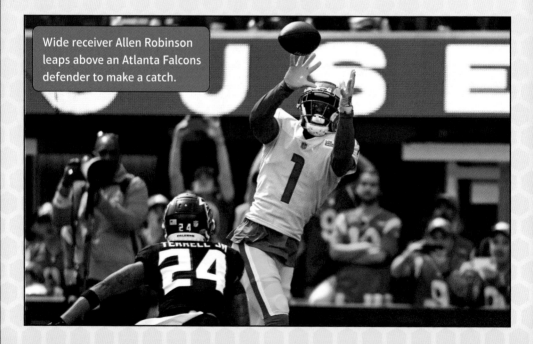

Wide receiver Allen Robinson leaps above an Atlanta Falcons defender to make a catch.

Aaron Donald was a Pro Bowl player after each of his first eight seasons from 2014 to 2021.

Todd Gurley scored 58 rushing touchdowns in his career with the Rams. He is tied for the most in team history with Marshall Faulk.

RAMS
SEASON RECORD
HOLDERS

RUSHING TOUCHDOWNS

1. Eric Dickerson, 18 (1983)
   Marshall Faulk, 18 (2000)
2. Todd Gurley, 17 (2018)
3. Greg Bell, 16 (1988)
4. Greg Bell, 15 (1989)

RECEIVING TOUCHDOWNS

1. Elroy Hirsch, 17 (1951)
2. Cooper Kupp, 16 (2021)
3. Harold Jackson, 13 (1973)
   Isaac Bruce, 13 (1995)
4. Isaac Bruce, 12 (1999)
   Torry Holt, 12 (2003)

PASSING YARDS

1. Matthew Stafford, 4,886 (2021)
2. Kurt Warner, 4,830 (2001)
3. Jared Goff, 4,688 (2018)
4. Jared Goff, 4,638 (2019)
5. Kurt Warner, 4,353 (1999)

RUSHING YARDS

1. Eric Dickerson, 2,105 (1984)
2. Eric Dickerson, 1,821 (1986)
3. Eric Dickerson, 1,808 (1983)
4. Steven Jackson, 1,528 (2006)
5. Jerome Bettis, 1,429 (1993)

PASS COMPLETIONS

1. Matthew Stafford, 404 (2021)
2. Jared Goff, 394 (2019)
3. Kurt Warner, 375 (2001)
4. Marc Bulger, 370 (2006)
   Jared Goff, 370 (2020)

SACKS

1. Aaron Donald, 20.5 (2018)
2. Robert Quinn, 19 (2013)
3. Kevin Carter, 17 (1999)
4. Kevin Greene, 16.5 (1988)
   Kevin Greene, 16.5 (1989)

GLOSSARY

conference: a group of sports teams that play against one another

cornerback: a defender whose main job is to prevent pass catches

defensive end: a player whose main jobs are to rush the quarterback and defend rushing plays

draft: when teams take turns choosing new players

drive: a series of plays by the offense in a football game

end zone: the area at each end of a football field where players score touchdowns

linebacker: a defender who usually plays in the middle of the defense

Pro Bowl: the NFL's all-star game

sack: when the quarterback is tackled for a loss of yards

trade: when teams exchange players or draft picks

turf: an artificial playing surface on some sports fields

LEARN MORE

Berglund, Bruce. *Football GOATs: The Greatest Athletes of All Time*. North Mankato, MN: Capstone, 2022.

Goodman, Michael E. *Los Angeles Rams*. Mankato, MN: The Creative Company, 2023.

Hill, Christina. *Aaron Donald*. Minneapolis: Lerner Publications, 2022.

Los Angeles Rams
https://www.therams.com

Pro Football Hall of Fame: Los Angeles Rams
https://www.profootballhof.com/teams/los-angeles-rams/

Sports Illustrated Kids—Football
https://www.sikids.com/football

INDEX

Bruce, Isaac, 23, 29

Dickerson, Eric, 21, 29

Dyson, Kevin, 16

Greatest Show on Turf,
The, 5, 16, 23

Gurley, Todd, 21, 29

Jones, Deacon, 20

Kupp, Cooper, 5-6, 25, 29

Olsen, Merlin, 20

SoFi Stadium, 5, 12

Stafford, Matthew, 5-6,
25-26, 29

St. Louis, Missouri, 12

Super Bowl, 5-6, 12, 15-17,
20, 23, 26

Warner, Kurt, 21, 23, 29

Washington, Kenny, 11

PHOTO ACKNOWLEDGMENTS

Image credits: MediaNews Group/Los Angeles Daily News via Getty Images/
Contributor/Getty Images, p.4; Cooper Neill/Contributor/Getty Images, p.6;
Andy Lyons/Staff/Getty Images, p.7; Vic Stein/Contributor/Getty Images, p.8;
Bettmann/Contributor/Getty Images, p.9; Bettmann/Contributor/Getty Images,
p.10; Bettmann/Contributor/Getty Images, p.11; DANIEL SLIM/Contributor/Getty
Images, p.12; Allen Kee/Contributor/Getty Images, p.13; JEFF HAYNES/Staff//
Getty Images, p.14; Focus On Sport/Contributor//Getty Images, p.15; Tom Hauck/
Staff/Getty Images, p.16; Mike Stobe/Contributor/Getty Images, p.17; Focus
On Sport/Contributor/Getty Images, p.18; Focus On Sport/Contributor/Getty
Images, p.19; Focus On Sport/Contributor/Getty Images, p.20; David Madison/
Contributor/Getty Images, p.21; Matthew Stockman/Staff/Getty Images, p.22;
George Gojkovich/Contributor/Getty Images, p.23; Focus On Sport/Contributor/
Getty Images, p.24; Michael Owens/Contributor/Getty Images, p.25; John McCoy/
Stringer/Getty Images, p.26; David Berding/Contributor/Getty Images, p.27;
Jayne Kamin-Oncea/Contributor/Getty Images, p.28

Design element: Master3D/Shutterstock.com.

Cover image: Thearon W. Henderson/Stringer/Getty Images